W9-CSB-681

Restorative Practices at School

An Educator's Guided Workbook to Nurture Professional Wellness,
Support Student Growth, and Build Engaged Classroom Communities

Becky McCammon

Text copyright © 2020 Becky McCammon. Design and concept copyright © 2020 Ulysses Press and its licensors. All rights reserved. Any unauthorized duplication in whole or in part or dissemination of this edition by any means (including but not limited to photocopying, electronic devices, digital versions, and the internet) will be prosecuted to the fullest extent of the law.

Published in the US by:
ULYSSES PRESS
P.O. Box 3440
Berkeley, CA 94703
www.ulyssespress.com

ISBN: 978-1-64604-000-1
Library of Congress Control Number: 2019951341

Printed in Canada by Marquis Book Printing
10 9 8 7 6 5 4 3 2 1

Acquisitions editor: Casie Vogel
Managing editor: Claire Chun
Editor: Renee Rutledge
Proofreader: Kathy Kaiser
Cover design: what!design @ whatweb.com
Cover artwork: © tachyglossus/shutterstock.com
Interior design: Jake Flaherty

NOTE TO READERS: This book is independently authored and published and no sponsorship or endorsement of this book by, and no affiliation with, any trademarked brands or other products mentioned within is claimed or suggested. All trademarks that appear in this book belong to their respective owners and are used here for informational purposes only. The authors and publisher encourage readers to patronize the quality brands mentioned in this book.

Contents

Who Is This Workbook Designed for and How Should I Use It?

The very first teacher I knew was my mother, Alice McCammon, an elementary educator with early childhood education and parent educator certificates/licenses. For my whole life, I have been immersed in the lexicon of learning and the value placed on being present with people. Because my mother's work with families acknowledged all that parents were learning simultaneously with their little ones, I believe I have always known that the greatest responsibility and joy of being an educator and adult is consistently examining my own learning needs so that I can be attuned to young people and the world they are experiencing freshly and frustratingly each day.

I am but one of many in the public education sphere attempting each day to bring my best self to school and to stay current with the needs of my students, as well as those of the dynamic, gifted adults who work in schools. I am not alone or original in my love for and tender faith in public education; I am most certainly not alone or distinguished in having a restorative mind-set and heart. I am neither expert nor infallible, but rather extraordinarily fortunate to have been blessed with a myriad of experiences these last twenty years in education, the last three of which I've served humbly as restorative practices program coordinator at St. Paul Public Schools.

At the 2019 American Federation of Teachers TEACH Conference, I heard author and educator Dr. Christopher Emdin, originator of #HipHopEd, speak. The way I understood his wisdom was that educators can feel brutalized by the wave of demands—from the system, the scope of their work, the constancy of harm, and beyond. Under such circumstances, where is the stillness needed to read something new, to consider and contemplate and then apply such learning?

For me, Emdin's wisdom rang deeply true. While I have book upon book stacked for my future reading and growth ambitions, my most engaged learning is from a journal of quotes I summon for my reflective practice and healing. Relevant to your reasons for engaging with this text, where is the space to take up restorative practices when the professional demands on those who work in schools are so great?

I've written this workbook to serve as a thoughtful opportunity and window for learning with restorative practices in schools or to continue to nurture a restorative learning path once a training has concluded. My intention is that this will serve as a tool even if the coach is hard to reach or if you're navigating a restorative instinct amid a school's conscious or unconscious dedication to nonrestorative ways of being.

This space is dedicated to all you know and are, so you might feel comfortable to try a 5-minute exploration, a 20-minute journal entry, or anything in between or beyond. Your engagement need not be sequential or linear unless you so choose.

So, set your coffee or LaCroix on this workbook because other work will call to you even as you consider your restorative hopes. Use your favorite pen or the one left behind in your classroom. Heck, I wish the book could smell like lavender so it might be soothing in that respect. Play in this. Feel free to write, scribble, annotate, highlight, and most vitally, reach out to me with questions because I'm all about relationships as my greatest inspiration for learning.

Your Restorative Lexicon: Embracing a Flexible Restorative Language

For 14 years, my craft was teaching English, so naturally, vocabulary exercises were something of my bread and butter. Later, I developed a more evolved approach (say, like chocolate babka) to my relationship with language and meaning.

When I first taught *To Kill a Mockingbird*, for example, I read and reread the book, believing that knowing it from every sequential plot moment would best prepare me to teach it. I would highlight words I imagined were "challenging" and assign those for students to define and use in a sentence. And yet, I know that we could have spent days and weeks exploring how words like "race," "bias," "fear," and even "girl" were used in the text. I wasn't wrong to imagine that learning "big" words has value but feel pretty sure I didn't always value words of exceptional meaning and depth.

Restorative practices (RP) in schools will hold different meaning and work from educator to educator, and there is no one definition of what this entails. A traditional workbook might launch into restorative practices as a matter of language, seeking to define it first and then inviting you to create your "own" sentences and practice from that definition. My invitation is for us, for you, to move toward a deeply personal place where your history and identity matter and are in direct relationship with all you seek to learn and unlearn in moving toward greater justice in your school community. This is at the heart of restorative practices—a way of being in tandem with habits and rituals.

The table of contents for this text is also designed in a way that speaks to the values inherent in restorative practices and the exercises build upon one another as a means to grow understanding—moving you from head to heart and heart to head in consideration of your journey as a restorative practitioner.

REFLECT: *What do you know about restorative practices?*

_____

_____

_____

_____

_____

What do you feel about restorative practices?

_____

_____

_____

_____

_____

What beliefs, hopes, and worries have brought you to this experience?

_____

_____

_____

_____

_____

We Are and I Am the Work

"I am the work." A remarkable artist named Shyam Bhagat shared this grounding, agitational, peaceful, and resolute phrase with learners at the 2019 National Association of Community and Restorative Justice Conference in Denver, Colorado.

I must own, first and foremost, the responsibility of my personal work—in my beliefs and practices and acts toward self-justice. I find peace in this locus of control and possibility, and still, the phrase propels me to do the internal work so that I might have a positive impact on relationships and systems.

I am the work.

It feels to me like this expression captures every responsibility, accountability, possibility, and measure of integrity I might apply to myself.

I am the work.

This book, this remarkably privileged invitation to share story with others, is the work.

As I was typing just now, my 9-year-old daughter, Lily, called to me from outdoors.

"Mom!" (pause)

"Becky!" (pause)

"McCammon!" (pause)

Motherhood is the work.

If you're reading this, **you are also the work**. And you're not alone.

Consider the ways I apply this term to my life:

I am the work because I am every day imperfect and always seeking to be more.

And **I am the work** in spite of some days feeling alone and worried that others are not working toward the same values and vision.

Being the work means taking responsibility, reflecting, and then not overreaching down a shame pathway.

Trusting to **my work** ahead feels frightening and exhausting and also, fortunately, there are still laundry and dishes to tend to and impulses to smile abundantly.

I am the work, anchored in the values of equity, growth, love, and relationship.

I am the work, inspired by the agape love in my life and a legacy of healthy and not-so-healthy relationships.

I am the work for my children, always and particularly, to be the kind of person I needed coming of age. I am someone's ancestor.

REFLECT: *Make a list of ways you are the work. Consider your relationships, your passions, and how your work has changed over time.*

_____

_____

_____

_____

_____

_____

_____

_____

_____

_____

Restorative practices underscore this truth: learning is relational. Two of my most remarkable teaching and learning partners are my children, Quinn and Lily, age 13 and 9, respectively.

Quinn's I Am the Work

I am the work if I put in the work.

I am the work when I am playing sports.

Being the work is like trying to open up a peanut butter jar.

The work is finishing a homework assignment before it is due.

I am the work trying to be in relationships and also, trying to solve misunderstandings.

I am the work when I go to school.

I am the work when I am in conflict with myself.

REFLECT: *What does this remind you of with your students?*

_____

_____

_____

_____

_____

With your adult peers?

_____

_____

_____

_____

_____

With your family and loved ones?

_____

_____

_____

_____

_____

Lily's I Am the Work

I am the work when I trust myself.

I am the work when I am helpful.

Being the work means asking for help when I need it.

The work is the most imperfect part of your most wonderful self.

I am the work when I feel included.

I am the work when I remember that if I am pretending to be someone else then I lose the best part of me.

I am the work when I remember that I am amazing

I am the work when I realize a new purpose.

REFLECT: *How are you walking around with your 9- and 13-year-old values in conflict, with care, and with both preservation and evolution?*

_____

_____

_____

_____

_____

REFLECT: *Compose your own "I am the work" piece. Feel free to play with the anaphoric sentence frames.*

I am the work _____

I am the work _____

Being the work _____

The work _____

I am the work _____

I am the work _____

I am the work _____

Belief

An educator is called to and chooses to work in schools because they believe in the inherent value, possibility, and brilliance of young people and also hold hope that education is a meaningful, powerful space for all. In the next invitation to compose, seek to center your students. For example, here's how my current role supporting twelve restorative practices pilot site schools and an additional eight implementation sites prompts me:

I am the work because within my practice and power is the opportunity to listen deeply to needs, hopes, and learning goals and respond with presence, integrity, and what next steps matter most.

And **I am the work** as someone who needs to consistently check and reconcile my position, title, and influence in relationship to how people feel they can show up with me authentically and I with them.

Being the work welcomes my learning curve and what I don't know blended with huge accountability and responsibility to know and share what I have organized of belief, value, and meaning.

The work is messy and gorgeous and familiar and straining and good—in my dang email folders and well beyond.

I am the work because I carry with me every professional and personal rubric that threatens to undo me simultaneously.

I am the work in harmony and discord with district, classroom, student, family, and community voices and relationships.

I am the work because I am not alone and seek to write and live a life my children can feel proud of.

REFLECT: *Where does this feel familiar?*

_____

_____

_____

_____

_____

What might happen in your school and personal life that prompts the harmony and discord mentioned?

_____

_____

_____

_____

_____

Your I Am the Work School–Centered Piece

For renewal, continued reflection, and support, consider returning to this exercise throughout the school year.

Example:

I am the work in September.

I am the work before winter break.

I am the work during testing season.

I am the work when the building is hot and students are tired....

I am the work because _____

And I am the work in spite of _____

Being the work means _____

Trusting to my work ahead feels _____

I am the work anchored in these values _____

I am the work inspired by _____

I am the work for _____ , always.

I am the work because _____

And I am the work in spite of _____

Being the work means _____

Trusting to my work ahead feels _____

I am the work anchored in these values _____

I am the work inspired by _____

I am the work for _____ , always.

I am the work because _____

And I am the work in spite of _____

Being the work means _____

Trusting to my work ahead feels _____

I am the work anchored in these values _____

I am the work inspired by _____

I am the work for _____ , always.

I am the work because _____

And I am the work in spite of _____

Being the work means _____

Trusting to my work ahead feels _____

I am the work anchored in these values _____

I am the work inspired by _____

I am the work for _____, always.

Sean is a poet. He identifies as African American and works in St. Paul Public Schools; his son Makai also attends St. Paul Public Schools.

I Am the Work

by Sean Stewart

I am the work of countless blood, sweat, and tears that water my spirit and reflect within the deep currents of the river of humanity.

I am the work of ancestral hands that sculpt the monuments of future generations.

Being the work is being that guiding force that seeks to restore one's self and others back to their traditional greatness.

The work *is* a revolutionary act that begins with a close examination of self and the learned behavior that I adopt as belief.

I am the work that seeks the interconnectedness of the world in the eyes of the child.

I am the work of the running river that flows continuously into the veins of future generations.

I am the work of healing the mind, body and *souls of black folk.*

REFLECT: *What meaningful imagery and feelings does Sean's piece inspire?*

_____

_____

_____

_____

_____

How might your work tie to what Sean's piece suggests?

_____

_____

_____

_____

_____

Valuing Your Authorship

The very first book I wrote was about the amazing and awesome experience of seeing Mary Lou Retton at a post-Olympics gymnastics event in the '80s (yes, I'm very much dating myself). Our teacher tasked us to be author, illustrator, and book binder.

I can still see the blue floral material purchased at a Joann Fabrics and Crafts store and sewed around the cardboard cover. I can visualize the pages where I carefully sought to merge a final draft or *good enough* version of both words and images, tentative steps toward being worthy of an audience.

I also attempted a brief foray into romantic fiction in fifth grade, where pencil scratching detailed a relationship with my school crush, Patrick. Of course, immature as both author and young person, I decided to show this whimsical masterpiece to all of my girlfriends, who giggled loudly and bantered about it most publicly at recess, which led to Patrick discovering my indiscreet folly and, oh, the embarrassment (and lesson about being selective with readers and tempering a desire for feedback).

My hope is that this book welcomes you as author, artist, and illustrator of a restorative story—for yourself, your students, and your school. Written words in book form have a permanence to them and still, more than ever, represent a temporary mirror and window for the world with new learning, refinements, and growth always taking place. My intention was to craft something flexible and responsive to your exploration of restorative practices that centers foremost your voice, your values, and your stories.

REFLECT: *Consider these memories: What do you recall about signing your name to something as author or artist? What thoughts run through your mind when you see books coauthored? What power and agency are you, as an educator, given to author your story in schools?*

Our Stories Often Involve Harm

Whether it's the little pigs' dear homes being scattered to the wind or someone being bullied into trying green eggs and ham, the tales we grow up with include harm and, more often than not, are absent an acknowledgment or repair of such injury.

My story about becoming a teacher has its origin in harm.

When I arrived at college, I knew I either wanted to be a teacher or a psychologist. I quickly learned that biology and experiences studying mice did not energize me. Rather, allying with young people in speech and theater at the nearby middle school and high school, and, later, in short teaching practicums in English gave me joy and purpose.

As a result, I aced my way through education courses and endured an English major awash in dead white men with a fitfully engaged and often rejecting attitude (I've fallen asleep on many a tome of Shakespeare, Chaucer, and Norton Anthology "fill in the blank"). Still, young people inspired me and so I knew the greatest content would be their learning journey.

What an unpleasant surprise then in the fall of my senior year to be invited by the chair of the English department for news that they didn't believe I was competent enough in English to teach. They recommended I take another semester of English courses and write a second senior paper.

I remember losing my breath—not suffocating, simply having my breath stolen.

I stayed for an extra semester because of that conversation and wrote another exhaustive senior paper. I rebelled against more English courses in favor of completing the English as a Second Language coursework. I graduated with a B– GPA and, aside from student teaching requirements, have never returned as an alumna to campus.

Some restorative practitioners, myself included, offer that restorative practices can find gentle summary in the idea that "hurt people hurt people." My story above speaks to the harms and practices that live in how we train educators, what we value in their giftedness, how we mentor and support each other, and what consistent strains and tensions live in our schools.

I don't believe the chair of the English department sought to harm me because they felt harmed; I believe the system cheated them from a way of being that would invite them to know my story and ask why I might be earning C's in Chaucer and Shakespeare or not attending class. I could have told them, but I was never asked.

This book seeks to invite questions of genuine care and hopefully, freeing reflection and healing.

REFLECT: *What values guide who you are as an educator and a person?*

_____

_____

_____

_____

_____

What practices might support being in healthy relationship with students, families, community, and yourself?

_____

_____

_____

_____

_____

What about restorative practices invite you and pique your interest to explore, practice, and imagine?

_____

_____

_____

_____

_____

Introducing Harm

Once upon a time a young person had a story. They met another young person who had their own story. Intrigued and curious about one another, they hoped to be friends. Turns out, living two different stories in a relationship meant that both infinite love and connection were possible, as well as conflict and the presence of Harm. And so one day, Harm happened upon the two of them and hurt them through words and actions. Harm did not want to apologize or make things right. The two friends held hands and walked through the Harm storm together and lived happily ever after.

REFLECT: *How does this brief fictional tale feel to you? In what ways does it feel deeply fictional or revealing?*

_____

_____

_____

_____

_____

What does it remind you of?

_____

_____

_____

_____

_____

What was it like to consider the idea of Harm as a character or antagonist outside young people?

_____

_____

_____

_____

_____

Between Harm's refusal and the young people choosing to mend their relationship, what could have happened?

_____

_____

_____

_____

_____

Given the opportunity to tailor and adapt the "Once Upon a Time" above, what does it feel critical to add?

_____

_____

_____

_____

_____

Our Perspectives and Practices Are Autobiographical

I grew up attending a Lutheran church in a suburb of the Twin Cities. An adoptee from Korea, I was one of a few children of color in the community and did not racially "match" visually. And my upbringing with a white family lent me familiarity with the cultural norms of a white community and congregation. In church, I knew that to be "good" was esteemed and to "sin," while natural, was something to seek forgiveness for. From the back of the sanctuary, the pastor would lead a call and response, which concluded with an idea that God forgives us our sins. This is how I understood the shape of repentance, an abstract forgiveness or "healing" after having properly, both internally and in a semianonymous chorus, named your sin.

REFLECT: *Growing up, when and where did you learn the concept of mistakes and the idea of forgiveness?*

_____

_____

_____

_____

_____

_____

_____

When might you have been invited to learn from your mistakes?

_____

_____

_____

_____

_____

_____

_____

When you were coming of age, who modeled values around "rule-breaking" and making it right?

_____

_____

_____

_____

_____

_____

_____

Lessons Learned Emerge
from All Stages of Life

My middle school years were like a coming-of-age tale of consistent fumbling. It was an era of so many questions and vexing or unknown answers, and it felt as if everyone were witnessing my struggle and embarrassment while clueless as to what was going on inside me. Lots of harm, with bangs.

In middle school I attended a summer sleepover camp for a week. I was attending on a scholarship, per usual, as life with a single mother had its distinct financial challenges. When we arrived and kids were sorting out their bags and unpacking, I saw a bag of gummy worms in someone's bag, my favorite treat. Impulsively, I took the bag of candy and hid it in my things. Instantly, I felt regret and wanted to undo my action. Unfortunately, within moments, the space filled with more campers and the theft was soon discovered. What occurred next was a blur of cries for justice, vilification of the character of whoever had stolen the candy, and threats of, "Whoever has taken it will be sent home." And so I felt trapped—I wanted to stay at camp and I didn't want my friends and fellow campers to hate me, yet I knew what I had done was wrong. I didn't see any way forward that allowed for me to learn from my mistake without a tinged reputation, leaving behind camp, and wandering through a pathway of shame. Because I wanted to be liked and to remain a part of the community, I chose silence (and telling the story publicly 30 years later).

REFLECT: *What about this story and experience resonates with you?*

_____

_____

_____

_____

_____

What feelings and beliefs does it connect to?

_____

_____

_____

_____

_____

These days it feels very much as if making a mistake means being marked as an outsider for good, that to misstep within a moment of poor (in)decision-making, forgetfulness, or dysregulation cancels out your value and goodness up until that moment.

REFLECT: *How does this idea, that we in education are often expected to be perfect in the midst of the very space that seeks to nurture learning fumbles in students, affect your sense of agency and worth?*

_____

_____

_____

_____

_____

How does this affect your practice with students?

_____

_____

_____

_____

_____

Restorative Practices at School

Restorative Allies and Supports

Sometimes, while I'm driving along and singing enthusiastically to the Top 40 radio station and it happens to be Wednesday or Saturday, I consider buying a lottery ticket. The temporary endorphin lift of imagining extraordinary wealth always gives me a few blocks' worth of glee where I imagine how I would share and gift such funds to my loved ones. This exercise, while based on the hopelessly fictional, grounds me in the relationships I have and what they mean to me.

So, the task for this page is simple: Tell someone about this learning. Tell someone that you're learning about self and about restorative practices. Post on Facebook or Twitter to see if anyone else is interested in reading or engaging with you on the topics shared in this book. Listen to your heart and stomach and mind as you field their responses. What came up for you? What came up for them?

Paying Attention to Our History of With

Picture a scene from your time as a student or as the educator, when group projects have just been introduced. What are the sounds, expressions, and physical responses to news of collaboration and teamwork assigned? (I'm grinning as I write this because so much of who I am surfaces and I become anxious at the idea of being held accountable to expectations in relationship to others.) Most importantly, what is your own response?

Learning as Relational

Consider the people in your life whom you learn from and with. What values and habits do they practice so that relational learning takes place? What about their way of being supports your openness to reflect, risk-take, and refine belief and/or practice?

MY LEARNING FROM AND WITH PARTNERS	THEIR VALUES AND HABITS
Quinn	Completely relationship driven. He will organize his route between classes to see important friends. In his football games, he is always the first to lend a hand to a teammate to help them up or to cheer them on.
Lily	Embraces her agency and power. When I remind her of required things like vaccinations, she will come back with, "You told me that if something makes me feel uncomfortable in my body that I can and should say no."

REFLECT: *What do you notice about the habits and practices of the relationships you learn most from and with?*

_____

_____

_____

_____

_____

_____

_____

_____

_____

If I could, I would have a merry conversation with every fabulous person who takes a chance on this book. I'd wish to learn about the three core values that describe you in your fullest, proudest self and when you last laughed in a way that made you feel alive and connected. Surely we would break bread together, because relationships are cemented over coffee, cake, and sublime crumbs—or dishes to your comfort and dietary needs.

In the exercise on the next page, think of your beloved friends and family and the rituals of breaking bread together that bind you in history, shared values, and relational consumption.

YOUR LOVED ONE	RITUAL MEAL	STORIES AND VALUES
Example: Longtime beloved friends Asha and Jen	Brie and bread Kale salad Puppy chow, a delicious blend of Chex, peanut butter, and chocolate	My culinary skills peak at wrapping cheese in foil and placing it with bread in the oven for messy, dippable fun. Jen is the salad master. Reminiscent of sleepovers from our youth, Asha makes puppy chow, shaking it up in paper bags. We each have our part and feast until we become progressively full through a meal prepared with love, steeped in our history of 30+ years of laughter and predictable comfort.

YOUR LOVED ONE	RITUAL MEAL	STORIES AND VALUES

EDUCATOR APPLICATION: *Consider your classroom and school practices around breaking bread or sharing meals together. How might these differ from practices around food in forming and maintaining relationships in your personal life? What might it look like to explore ritualized meal preparation, shared food, storytelling, and similar ways of community building with your colleagues and students?*

STUDENTS/COLLEAGUES	RITUAL MEAL	STORIES AND VALUES

Critical Pause

September in schools feels a certain kind of way. The days before a fall break or family conferences in November all hold familiar feelings for educators. The week leading up to winter break is a unique blend of exhaustion and adrenaline. Within all of these seasons and Sunday-evening kinds of feelings, restorative practices invite habits that support our healthiest selves.

For this page, take a breath. Draw what breathing has felt like today. Think about a song that always lets you exhale. Play it, on repeat. Then, pause. Consider your relationship to pausing. What values do you assign to that practice?

Knowing Your Whole Self

An educator's potential internal monologue: Um, so, I'm 31 pages into the book and this has focused entirely on self. When will we get to the circles I keep hearing about? About what restorative practices in schools look like?

An author's reassurance: Soon. And, restorative practices are deeply about who we are in relationship to others, places, history, and systems. Restorative practices invite a depth of introspection so that learning and planning and implementation come from us, rather than being done to us. And, this book is dedicated to the individual work of lifting up our greatest strengths and hopes toward a restorative impulse and restorative practices in our lives and classrooms.

Below is an exercise experienced and then borrowed with grace from brilliant members of the St. Paul Public Schools Equity Team. You will find five circles. With care, place a primary descriptor/part of your identity in each one of the circles. For example, I would include the following: Educator, Mother, Woman of Color, Learner, and Hopeful Changemaker. Each of these descriptions holds unique import and value to me.

Consider your process for identifying the core aspects of your identity.

Next to each circle, compose your "why" for selecting what you did, or words, values, and ideas that come to mind. Infuse your writing with the dimension and scope that celebrate the fullness of that category of who you are.

For example, I am a mother because each day when I wake and each evening when I fall asleep, my children are the heartbeats and breath I am most concerned with. My greatest rubric for each day is, "How well and lovingly did I 'mom'?"

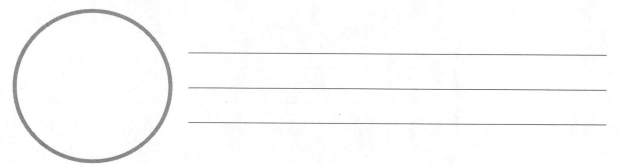

Next, consider being forced to eliminate one circle of your personhood. Which would you choose, and how would you choose it? Know that I appreciate the complexity of this process and invitation, so in your discomfort, please know the intent of this question is to examine what comes up for you when one of your identity "limbs" is harmed—not to cause harm.

As you breathe deeply through such a choice and reflection—even an imagined one—picture an experience where someone has to select one of your core parts of self to eliminate or harm. What injury do they experience in that act of limiting who you are?

When I first experienced this exercise, the facilitator, a kind and loving person, held space for our reflections and responses. Not shockingly, the idea of reducing or doing away with a core part of ourselves was wrenching. The idea that someone else would restrict our full selves was even more painful. The facilitator's question was this: What about school policy and our own personal practices limits and tells students immediately upon entering school that they need to leave behind some part of their true selves?

On this page are many circles. Consider your school and classroom. Which identity markers are invited, welcomed, and most supported? Place those ideas and truths in each of the circles.

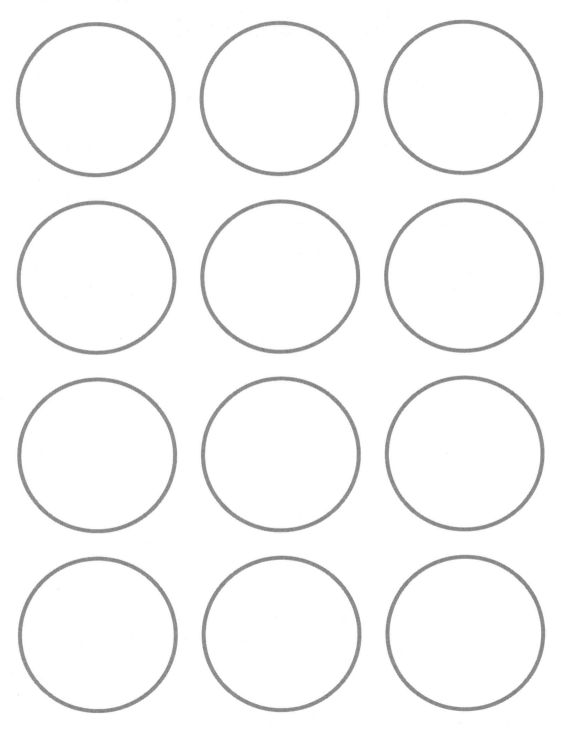

Restorative Practices at School

Examining Systems from Our Identity and Values

Across the country, school districts and buildings have their own versions of a rights and responsibilities handbook or the rules that guide adult actions when kids are kids—in their good, in their messy, and in their harm, in learning, and beyond.

Human resources offices also have an equally elusive handbook that guides when adults misstep.

In both cases and spaces, I have witnessed these guides perpetuate additional harm to adults and young people.

Answer the following questions in the table below:

What harm have you seen or witnessed and how does it affect you? And where, in the midst of these responses, do you see spaces for young people and adults to embrace their "work" and opportunities to work *with*? For reference, see We Are and I Am the Work on page 5, and Paying Attention to Our History of With on page 24.

YOUTH	ADULTS

Example: I have witnessed schools that announce that any student in the hallways after the bell rings will receive an automatic detention. This is deeply upsetting because it means that students hear first an absolute rule rather than a value: We want you in class. It means too that a young person with health issues or needs—whether they occur monthly or are brought about by breakfast—must worry about bathroom trips in between class and fear having to explain themselves to an adult or face punishment. My work is to brave the challenging conversation with leadership teams to understand the value to such a policy and offer my perspective on the systematized harm possible under such a practice.

What Are Restorative Practices?

Restorative practices are the belief that learning is relational and our interconnectedness and inherent value are linked; it is the work of unpacking, revealing, and healing ways of being in school and life.

Restorative practices must commit to racial equity and acknowledging a history of harm and injustice that is persistently present and profound in our schools each day. Restorative practices are antiracist work, are the work of decolonizing our schools and reconciling how we all hurt and how some inherit a legacy of loss and injustice.

Restorative practices capture the consistent journey of getting acquainted, establishing relationships, addressing issues, and developing action plans and a shared future tense.

Collective perspectives via the Minnesota Department of Education Restorative Practices resources offer this definition: Restorative practices are drawn from the traditions of indigenous people and communities of color around the world. They are grounded in a belief that people are profoundly relational, interconnected, and inherently good. Restorative practices include ways of creating community that honor the importance of relationships among all members of the community, as well as practices to repair relationships when harm has been caused and address the needs of all people impacted by the harm.

Restorative practices represent the ways in which we give our humanity presence in the midst of a complex story of public education.

Restorative practices invite a renewal and cultivation of our best selves, with habits and practices in constant development. It is the steady work of trusting that we are enough. For educators in ever-adapting, challenging circumstances, this means being enough to create a community of belonging and a space where equity is more than aspirational and indeed is a critical wrestling with and an adaptation of practice.

While public educators are currently tasked with an accelerated and unending cycle of learn, internalize, and apply, restorative practices are perhaps the most profound invitation to school communities to pause, breathe, and proceed with reverence for relationships over rules and equity at center.

On the pages that follow, engage with how these varied, meaningful definitions look, sound, and feel to you. What about each one resonates? How might students read and experience these ideas and definitions? How might each one be composed in student-friendly language? And how do you see these definitions blending and collaborating with one another?

Restorative practices are the belief that learning is relational and our interconnectedness and inherent value are linked; it is the work of unpacking, revealing, and healing ways of being in school and life.

Restorative practices capture the consistent journey of getting acquainted, establishing relationships, addressing issues, and developing action plans and a shared future tense.

While public educators are currently tasked with an accelerated and unending cycle of learn, internalize, and apply, restorative practices are perhaps the most profound invitation to school communities to pause, breathe, and proceed with reverence for relationships over rules and equity at center.

Restorative practices invite a renewal and cultivation of our best selves, with habits and practices in constant development. It is the steady work of trusting that we are enough. For educators in ever-adapting, challenging circumstances, this means being enough to create a community of belonging and a space where equity is more than aspirational and indeed, is a critical wrestling with and an adaptation of practice.

Restorative practices represent the ways in which we give our humanity presence in the midst of a complex story of public education.

Restorative practices must commit to racial equity and acknowledging a history of harm and injustice that is persistently present and profound in our schools each day. Restorative practices are anti-racist work, are the work of decolonizing our schools and reconciling how we all hurt and how some inherit a legacy of loss and injustice.

Our Value Origins

The circle of perspectives offered on page 37 have indigenous origin and present-tense truth. Each of our identities emerges from a meaningful beginning, reconciled with our day-to-day reality. In my story, I was five months old when I was adopted from Korea. I believe that my parents held the value of family. I was their first child after an emotional journey with infertility. I believe they held the values of hope and patience.

As an adoptee, I hold dear to the value that family is born of generous, welcoming, and forgiving love.

When I gave birth to my son, Quinn, the first biological relative I had known, and looked into his eyes, the value I held dear was one of mirror and belonging to someone more powerfully than I had ever experienced before. Now, I revel in the value of hearing people say, "You look so much like one another," and this familiarity holds new definition and meaning for me.

Every sentence, interaction, and story is steeped in values potentially subtle, profound, expressed, or absent. Values originate from our coming-of-age with family, among friends, and in our faith communities, from our opening days as students through what choices and experiences prompt our work in and relationship to schools.

Restorative practices invite and welcome an examination of your values and the gifts and stories you bring to school each day—and how your values represent space for hope, patience, and belonging.

In sharing my story of origin and birth, there are values held and expressed. In believing that I am composing a (hopefully) supportive text for other educators that could be meaningful to an individual's exploration and potential implementation of restorative practices, there are values actualized. In leaving much to an educator's imagination, self-discipline, and artistry, there is a confirmation that educators are vibrantly dedicated to transformative change for and with our students, families, peers, and schools.

Value in story. Value in creation. Value in assurances of one's good.

REFLECT: *For you, what do these ideas bring up?*

Our Creative Expression of Values

With educators across St. Paul I have led the following exercise: Using dry spaghetti and marshmallows, build an image of the value or values you bring to school with you each day. What do you think you would build and how would you describe it to young people? Feel free to draw in the space below too.

And just for fun, what about dry spaghetti and marshmallows feels a bit like school?

_____

_____

_____

EDUCATOR APPLICATION: *If you were to try this exercise with students, what value might they find in it? What modifications do you anticipate you might wish to make? What values would you need to embrace to take this leap with students?*

Our Relationships Hold Distinct Values

Think of loved ones in your life through the lens of their values, your values, and shared values.

Name	Without even trying, these values are always present	When there is struggle or challenge, these values are present	The values I seek to bring to my interactions with loved ones in both of those truths, and my restorative reasoning
Rebecca	Curiosity, a zeal for learning	Integrity, elevation of equity	Listening, affirmation, encouragement of self-care

Now, consider your students. Select 12 students that come to mind. List their names below.

Name	Without even trying, these values are always present	When there is struggle or challenge, these values are present	The values I seek to bring to my interactions with the scholar in both of those truths, and my restorative reasoning
1.			
2.			
3.			
4.			
5.			
6.			

Name	Without even trying, these values are always present	When there is struggle or challenge, these values are present	The values I seek to bring to my interactions with the scholar in both of those truths, and my restorative reasoning
7.			
8.			
9.			
10.			
11.			
12.			

REFLECT: *What did you notice about the consistent values you bring to relationships?*

_____

_____

_____

_____

_____

What can you rightfully, wonderfully celebrate about your awesomeness?

_____

_____

_____

_____

As you delved into the values your students bring naturally, what did you notice?

_____

_____

_____

_____

What about your practice and community might wonderfully celebrate student awesomeness?

_____

_____

_____

_____

What about strain and challenge brings forth different values (truth, fight, flight, or freeze, for example)? For yourself and for your students?

_____

_____

_____

_____

Consider your colleagues at school.

Name	Without even trying, these values are always present	When there is struggle or challenge, these values are present	The values I seek to bring to my interactions with my colleague in both of those truths, and my restorative reasoning

Foundational, Shared Understanding

Picture a favorite tree from your childhood or present-day landscape. When your engagement with this text began, your understanding for restorative practices might have been represented by the tree as it presents aboveground, with varied branches and leaves of nuanced shape.

Because we have lived in different spaces, what trees we picture are likely varied. And still, I assume that we share a "sense" of what a tree looks like.

A handful of colloquial phrases include the language of assumption. "Making an assumption makes an ass of you and me" is a popular one. In many of the meetings I attend and teams of which I am a part, we are guided to "assume positive intentions." Both of these expressions, from my perspective, reduce the role of and our relationships to assumptions amid the realities of bias, equity, and values.

Here are some unhealthy assumptions made about me over the years:

- That I do not speak English.
- That the "Which Asian country are you from?" game is fun for me to engage in.
- That my quietness or pauses signal a compliant nature.
- That when I seek to question norms within a space, team, or system, I am inherently oppositional and comfortable with holding an isolated position/perspective.

Here are some healthier assumptions I embrace:

- I came of age loved by others and am still in healthy relationships with amazing people.
- That I am a learner, always, and seeking to grow and be the best me.
- That I make mistakes and pay attention to what those moments teach me.
- That each time I raise my voice to question or interject an absent narrative—a perspective not historically considered or included, especially if someone from that affinity group is not present—I am taking a risk, and while steady in my personal integrity, it comes at a cost.

Examining Our Assumptions

What are some unhealthy assumptions that have been made about you over the years?

1. _____

2. _____

3. _____

4. _____

What are some healthier assumptions about you that you embrace and welcome?

1. _____

2. _____

3. _____

4. _____

REFLECT: *How have these assumptions shaped your identity both personally and professionally? How have you dynamically learned to process harmful assumptions and bias and, conversely, empower healthier ones?*

_____

_____

_____

_____

_____

As a student, what did you assume was the purpose of school?

Now that you work in schools, what do you believe to be a school's purpose?

What contemporary assumptions about school affect your day-to-day work?

What about your work each day challenges and upends these assumptions?

And now to the Seven Core Assumptions of restorative practices, as humbly shared in the text *Circle Forward* by Carolyn Boyes-Watson and Kay Pranis.

Seven Core Assumptions

What we believe to be true

1 The true self in everyone is good, wise, and powerful.

2 The world is profoundly interconnected.

3 All human beings have a deep desire to be in a good relationship.

4 All human beings have gifts, and everyone is needed for what they bring.

5 Everything we need to make positive change is already here.

6 Human beings are holistic.

7 We need practices to build habits of living from the core self.

In the table below, use your own words to reflect on your relationship with the Seven Core Assumptions.

CORE ASSUMPTION	VALUE AGREEMENT	VALUE TENSION
The true self in everyone is good, wise, and powerful.	Example: At our core, I believe people come from innocence, are always learning, and have the potential to create positive change.	Example: Sometimes the patterned behavior of people who create harm with their words and actions makes it very difficult to believe they are wise or good.
The true self in everyone is good, wise, and powerful.		
The world is profoundly interconnected.		
All human beings have a deep desire to be in a good relationship.		
All human beings have gifts, and everyone is needed for what they bring.		
Everything we need to make positive change is already here.		
Human beings are holistic.		
We need practices to build habits of living from the core self.		

Remember how I suggested that you have a partner or learning friend for this experience? Here's a space for intentional exchange with someone you love or a trusted work friend. What do they believe or feel about the Seven Core Assumptions?

CORE ASSUMPTION	VALUE AGREEMENT	VALUE TENSION
The true self in everyone is good, wise, and powerful.		
The world is profoundly interconnected.		
All human beings have a deep desire to be in a good relationship.		
All human beings have gifts, and everyone is needed for what they bring.		
Everything we need to make positive change is already here.		
Human beings are holistic.		
We need practices to build habits of living from the core self.		

EDUCATOR APPLICATION: *If you shared this with your students, what would they offer of their wisdom and insight?*

CORE ASSUMPTION	VALUE AGREEMENT	VALUE TENSION
The true self in everyone is good, wise, and powerful.		
The world is profoundly interconnected.		
All human beings have a deep desire to be in a good relationship.		
All human beings have gifts, and everyone is needed for what they bring.		
Everything we need to make positive change is already here.		
Human beings are holistic.		
We need practices to build habits of living from the core self.		

Pause for All the Ways We Experience Joy

Earlier in the book, I referenced my affection for grand Top 40 pop sing-alongs in the car. During a particularly stressful morning, a friend guided me to "This Is Me" by Keala Settle, from the soundtrack of *The Greatest Showman*. The song quickly made its way into my rotation of musical support.

Below, explore the idea of a restorative playlist that celebrates and honors the complexity of the Seven Core Assumptions of restorative practices. What will you design and how might these songs make their way into your classroom or school? What playlist might students be invited to create to link to these themes and beliefs?

CORE ASSUMPTION	MUSICAL SELECTIONS
The true self in everyone is good, wise, and powerful.	Idea: "This Is Me" by Keala Settle
The world is profoundly interconnected.	
All human beings have a deep desire to be in a good relationship.	
All human beings have gifts, and everyone is needed for what they bring.	
Everything we need to make positive change is already here.	
Human beings are holistic.	
We need practices to build habits of living from the core self.	

Our Stories Matter

For as long as I can remember, I have sought to be good or to be good enough. My understanding of where babies come from was sourced this way: good people got to have babies and thus found themselves pregnant. What a pickle of a situation then to imagine that at any moment, my goodness might result in an unexpected gift.

My tale of deep naivete points to what felt like a chasm of confusion for my coming-of-age morality. If the ideal was to be good, what about the alternative? What if I was drawn to a behavior or experience that wasn't good? What if someone hurt my feelings or harmed me? What was that in relationship to not being good enough?

Restorative practices have supported a way to reconcile how I experience harm as a good (enough) person and what to do in those moments when my response feels not-so-ideal. Goodness isn't permanent and yet, harm does feel very much constant in its varied forms. So, what then?

REFLECT: *What are some tales from your childhood of your goodness and quest for goodness?*

_____

_____

_____

_____

_____

_____

_____

_____

_____

_____

_____

What was the learning of these moments and how has that stayed with you?

_____

_____

_____

_____

_____

_____

_____

_____

_____

_____

Today, which core assumption did you lean into deeply and how did that feel? Was there a core assumption that you struggled with and what could support look like tomorrow?

1 The true self in everyone is good, wise, and powerful.

7 We need practices to build habits of living from the core self.

2 The world is profoundly interconnected.

6 Human beings are holistic.

3 All human beings have a deep desire to be in a good relationship.

5 Everything we need to make positive change is already here.

4 All human beings have gifts, and everyone is needed for what they bring.

Harm and Needs

One way we've prefaced thinking about restorative practices is that "Hurt people hurt people," and that's neither the end of the story nor the entire story. What comes up for you when you read this expression?

I first experienced these series of prompts during a one-day Introduction to Restorative Practices offered by the Minnesota Department of Education.

Think back to a recent time you felt harmed. In that harm, what did you need? Why do you believe you needed those things?

Think of a recent time when you caused harm. In that harm, what did you need? Why do you believe you needed those things?

Examine your list of needs for when you felt harmed. Reflect on your needs when you caused harm. What do you notice? What stands out to you? What needs are most typically met and in which scenario? Which needs most often go unmet?

Consider your classroom and school community. How are the practices and policies of the adults in school designed to meet the needs of scholars who experience harm and who might cause harm? What about your personal relationship to harm and your needs might affect your response when students feel or cause harm?

REFLECT: *This exercise began with the phrase, "Hurt people hurt people." What could it look, sound, and feel like for your family, friends, or classroom to explore this idea together?*

_____

_____

_____

_____

_____

What needs might be met through this collaboration and dialogue?

_____

_____

_____

_____

_____

From Harm to Hope

For the remainder of the book, you'll be introduced to some vulnerable and brave people in my circle of learning and restorative practices. Their tales are offered for reflection, inspiration, and support in partnership toward the continued elevation of the Seven Core Assumptions.

Circle and Centerpiece

The stories that follow will include reference to circle, an indigenous process that seeks to invite and value our voices with equity. In a circle, a talking piece is used to signify who may speak from their heart, their truth, and with respect. A person can always, always choose to pass the talking piece and a circle keeper consistently observes when an additional "round" or "pass" might be needed. Circle begins foundationally with community building, getting acquainted and creating relationship in collective values and agreements. Circles may support addressing issues, problem solving, or repairing harm when partnered with meaningful preparation and preconferencing. Circle, most especially when it seeks to repair and restore relationship and community, must be voluntary. Circles invites a depth of listening practice and slowing down that can bring forth the Seven Core Assumptions. Content circles, or those that specifically lean into academic content or new learning, believe that through community we learn and have capacity to move through much "material."

Additionally, the language of a centerpiece in circle will be introduced. The original centerpiece of circle was that of fire; communities gathered around fire for warmth, safety, and connection. In contemporary circles, a centerpiece is a visual anchor for the values of the community. A centerpiece invites our gaze and focus as we speak and listen and ideally holds items or artifacts precious to the students, adults, and circle keeper.

The following is a restorative tale of harm and repair from a restorative practices elementary school. It is shared in its original form and language of the circle keeper.

We had the most powerful circle with our head custodian, Mr. K., a gentle giant at 6 foot plus. The kids adore him. He came to RP 101 on a Saturday, the whole day. He encouraged his custodial team to join us on the makeup day and arranged for them to be paid to come. In the lunchroom when he's cleaning, he's always interacting with kids. They like to see his muscles; he used to be a paramedic. He shared at the training, "I don't know much about teaching, but I sure like how we ask the kids how they feel." And so he knew about the RP work, and he values it.

And then comes the middle of the year, and we had some bathroom issues that became a big problem. I invited Mr. K to come and we held the circle with each group of the third-, fourth-, and fifth-grade boys.

I led the circle and had him share some of what was happening and the impact. He came from the perspective that there was no blame. He said, "We all take such pride, this is our home, and I take such pride in making the school beautiful and safe for all of us." Then he took the perspective of his team and told us how they would skip their dinner break just to make sure everything was cleaned up, and they would go home late. I interjected at times to ask questions, like what time he started in the morning (5 a.m.) and what time his staff got home at night (10:30 p.m.), and so forth. Then I asked what steps it would take to remove urine from the walls and floor. He literally shared from his heart his pride of the custodial team and how much he loved the building.

You could have heard a pin drop because the boys had never made that connection between their antics and the man that they really adored—it's just really funny to them to pee on the floor and walls. Right afterward, my prompt was, "Now hearing that, can you just share how you feel?" We talked about this not being a blaming, but a circle to talk about how to make it better. The next prompt was, "What's one thing you can do to help this?"

They took it to heart. All week long there were kids coming up to me, telling me they picked up paper towels off the floor, turned off running water, saying by all of that, "We are watching." And one of the boys who is not that fluent in English talked so emotionally about it, saying, "I just don't understand how you would come into someone's house and pee on the floor. That just makes me so mad." It was so hard for him to articulate, but he did it so powerfully.

The last prompt of that circle was, "How do you feel now?" They heard Mr. K say, "I feel so hopeful." It was one hundred times better than I had anticipated in terms of the outcome, and it came from the heart. You could see the impact in the faces. It went so well that we did it proactively with our first-grade boys about bathroom usage.

REFLECT: *For you, what does this story illustrate?*

_____

_____

_____

_____

_____

What could have gone differently?

_____

_____

_____

_____

_____

What is your role as an adult in school to interrupt and pause before cycling your professional or personal hurt, or—in the case of this story—feeling disrespected by student behavior?

_____

_____

_____

_____

_____

Our Good, Wise, and Powerful Educator Neighbors

Life as an educator is often shaped and remembered in small chunks of time, equivalent to that of passing time between bells at school. Whether it's three minutes of magic working one on one with a scholar, three minutes of zen observing young people in collaborative good, or three minutes in the hallway with your educator next-door neighbor. Those three minutes link like a restorative garland on challenging days and seasons.

For me, being language arts neighbors with Nicki Ramos was full of light and care. Her ferocious nature as a learner and passionate student advocate was an enduring inspiration and support for me.

Here are some of her restorative details. Nicki identifies as a white female and uses she/her/hers pronouns. She teaches language arts to middle school scholars.

The core values Nicki has seen strengthened in school in relationship to RP are listening, compassion, authenticity, and honesty.

These are her words:

> *Restorative practices have always been a part of who I strive to be as a facilitator in the classroom: circles and community building and holding each other accountable in compassionate ways. Over my past 14 years of teaching, I have learned more about the pedagogical "beef" behind why restorative practices are so vital to the health of our communities. I have learned the ways in which I am susceptible to falling back into my white privilege as well, even though I say I am being restorative. I have learned how my start as an educator began with me holding a "white savior" complex. I needed to hold onto my love of learning and love of working with families, but I needed to reframe my narrative around my students and their families. Trauma-based learning, racial equity work, restorative practices, and Montessori pedagogy became my pillars as an educator.*
>
> *I've learned language to help me to challenge myself and others when we step back into easy criticism and discipline WITHOUT a restorative mind-set. Each year that I stay in our public education system, I am surprised by the cycle of stress we go through each school year. We begin our years with excitement and community love, but so quickly we get stressed and rushed and we so easily go back to traditional and harmful practices that don't serve the whole person! Consequently, educators are not taking care of ourselves as we should be and we are not able to serve our kids and families as we should be. We have to remember to slow down and make time for each other. This is why I am so proud to be an educator in a district and in*

an educators' union that has made RP a priority. We must keep it a priority and keep ourselves accountable to being TRULY restorative, to best serve our families in St. Paul. We can't ever stop learning and challenging each other, especially when it comes to restorative practices.

To me, restorative practices are not about paling the color of truth or adding glitter to what harm is before us. Restorative practices invite genuine reflection and investigation when new strategies create the same impact as our old ways and models of doing things.

In her thoughtful integrity, Nicki also offers this wisdom:

I recently witnessed adults as circle keepers at the end of our school year who had not had any RP training and had very minimal experience with participating in RP circles. As a result, great damage was caused. Those circles were held to repair harm, but the keeper facilitated the circle in such a way that actually caused more hurt to each party. The circle keeper minimized the harm that participants expressed, spoke over participants, and took sides, among other behaviors. As a result, participants felt angry, expressed that they experienced racist acts within circle, felt dismissed, and, accordingly, felt disdain for restorative practices and restorative circles. I heard from both students and adults who had participated in these negative circles and I felt anger and frustration as a result. I struggled with how to support those involved. What was the best way to advocate for those harmed? What was the best way to challenge the circle keepers, who had further exacerbated the harm? Trust and relationships were broken after these circles occurred and the circle keepers seemed completely unaware and unconcerned with the harm they had caused. I know one thing we can do is continue to share the great importance of having training and experience before being a circle keeper.

REFLECT: *Having recently considered the vibrant needs and complexity of harm, what do you take from Nicki's sharing of harm that could occur under the auspices of exploring and implementing restorative practices?*

_____

_____

_____

_____

What mind-set, preparation, and guidance could ensure that efforts to address harm do not perpetuate it?

_____

_____

_____

_____

_____

Some of the defining features of the circle keepers and restorative school practitioners I have met are those are grace, patience, and thoughtful welcome. This is profoundly true of Ann Hite, a longtime educator who centers perspective taking, listening, and speaking with respect in her circles and work.

Her description of a beloved talking piece reminds me powerfully of our timeless goodness.

> *I often use a small plastic picture frame with photos of my daughters taken just after their births in the hospital. Each photo is accompanied by another photo of them in their early 20s. When I first used this as a talking piece, I explained how these photos have been an ongoing reminder to me that every student (no matter how challenging) is someone's precious baby. More recently, I have talked about how much I learn from my daughters and how important it is to me to have their energy and strength in circle and how I believe that the healing power of circle is given back to them through my participation.*

REFLECT: *What values and feelings emerge for you when you think about your days as a baby versus today?*

_____

_____

_____

_____

_____

How does that sense of having grown up show up in your classroom practices and way of being?

_____

_____

_____

_____

_____

In your classroom, what are the objects and reminders of young people's innocence and the gift of growing up imperfectly?

_____

_____

_____

_____

In your home, what are these fixed reminders?

_____

_____

_____

_____

Ann identifies as a white woman and uses she/her/hers pronouns. This circle story seems fitting to the idea of our youth, growth, and coming-of-age vibrantly energizing one another and our community:

> Two students who had been friends since preschool began growing apart ungracefully, causing a lot of pain to each other and their parents. All six (two students and four parents) agreed to hold a circle with administration and behavioral staff. They shared their strengths, sadness, and tears. After circle, parents hugged, and several days later, the students were seen skipping and laughing down the hall.

REFLECT: *How did you learn that some relationships have a permanence in your life?*

_____

_____

_____

_____

_____

How did you learn about those relationships that are substantive, but perhaps for shorter periods of time?

_____

_____

_____

_____

_____

What critical social emotional learning is tied to that cycle of loss, grief, and an openness to new relationships?

_____

_____

_____

_____

_____

In your classroom or school space, how are students guided through these phases of building relationships, creating trust, and, at times, experiencing harm?

_____

_____

_____

_____

How are students and adults encouraged to reexamine friendship or connection with new habits or practices?

_____

_____

_____

_____

What habits or practices might your whole class or school engage in to support the values of dynamic, ever-changing relationships?

_____

_____

_____

_____

_____

What might individual coaching of young people or your peers look and sound like?

_____

_____

_____

_____

_____

The Wisdom of Departing from the Familiar

One of our restorative practices pilot sites, a high school, shared this tale in a listening circle/focus group. I now share it with you for your reflection.

> *The way I use [RP] is just try to bring students' experience and emotions into something that doesn't naturally have that: physics and aerospace. I've been really trying to get kids to talk about their experiences, emotions, and feelings as doing so pertains to things we're talking about. That's new since we started RP, especially the emotions. Until this year, I've never asked kids those things. We were doing an aerodynamics unit, and I asked them to imagine flying a kite and what were the feelings and emotions they were having while flying a kite. And we connected the feelings to forces and then the forces to the way the kite moves. We weren't writing it but it was a primer piece so we could refer back to "remember when we talked about the kite?'" And recently with energy, we started with, "What are emotions that are high energy? What are emotions that are low energy?" And we used those comparisons to try to come up with definitions for what energy is. It was cool: "High energy is rage, happiness, and excitement. Low energy is peace, calm, and depression." So, it went deep. I don't know if it is having value in their understanding but it is way more interesting to teach. It's not just, "Do you know this, yes or no?" I'm trying to personalize it and connect it.*

REFLECT: *Restorative practices are often introduced to communities as a way to address harm and "deal" with behaviors. What about this story refines or builds on your understanding of restorative work in schools?*

_____

_____

_____

_____

_____

_____

_____

_____

The story on page 75 includes an example of a content circle, an experience that leans into community relationship and experience to elevate and energize academic content. What about this story inspires personal connection and reflection about your practice?

_____

_____

_____

_____

_____

_____

_____

_____

_____

_____

EDUCATOR APPLICATION: *What emotions and values do you attach to high energy? To low energy? In experiencing students and staff with high or low energy, what comes up for you?*

_____

_____

_____

_____

_____

_____

_____

_____

All of Our Wisdom

I grew up on Star Wars movies, big time. In these films, there is a critical relationship between the Jedi (wise ones) and Padawans (apprentices); Jedis determine the apprentice's readiness or skill and how much wisdom they have acquired in training. Much of the same dynamic can exist in schools between veteran and newer educators. A culture of "respect your elders" can twist unfortunately to suggest that age and length of experience are the key prerequisites for wisdom, leaving students and even some adults consistently in the role of Padawan.

REFLECT: *Where did you learn what it means to be wise?*

_____

_____

_____

_____

_____

What values do you most often partner with wisdom?

_____

_____

_____

_____

_____

In contrast, what values or identity markers do you feel discouraged from pairing with the idea of wisdom?

_____

_____

_____

_____

_____

How does the value of wisdom live in your school community?

_____

_____

_____

_____

_____

In your classroom?

_____

_____

_____

_____

_____

How is student wisdom treated? Explain.

_____

_____

_____

_____

_____

If you were to develop a scale of stages toward the achievement of wisdom, how would you design such a rubric? Educators, for example, are often evaluated as Below Standard, Developing, Proficient, and Distinguished.

Use the templates that follow to craft some wisdom scales.

Super wisdom, at 100, includes Yoda, the musician Lizzo, and the result of being consistently well fed and rested. What else marks where wisdom emerges or where it is absent? Mark these attributes of wisdom where you see them emerging on the wisdom scale below. Use the text space to describe your wisdom metric.

SUPER
WISDOM:
Well fed,
rested

```
0    10    20    30    40    50    60    70    80    90    100
```

_____

_____

_____

_____

Where wisdom is equivalent to being well loved, who has wisely dedicated their heart to loving you and on what sort of scale?

PERSONS

Example: Lily and Quinn

SCALE

Infinitely wise because they name their love for me daily coupled with "feedback" about my areas of growth as a mom.

_____

_____

_____

_____

_____

Reflect on the image below; what about wisdom emerges from unexpected events, from both the good and the challenge of life?

Below, design an image or series of images that show the relationship between students and how they come to see or trust themselves as wise. What inspired your representation of wisdom in youth?

Now, construct a timeline of your ages through the years and strive to include markers of your wisdom at each stage. What about such an invitation prompts discomfort? What was easy or comfortable about this exercise?

Our Relationship to Advice

I love my advice in the form of story. I like when it comes discreetly and preferably in a physically comfortable space when I am well fed and rested. I like advice offered with humility and in relationship.

I also love a good haiku.

The art to advice

Lies always with the intent

Of relationship.

REFLECT: *Consider advice that has been meaningful and relational. What about its offerings felt positive, engaging, and free from bias? What relationship is there, for you, between advice and learning?*

_____

_____

_____

_____

_____

EDUCATOR APPLICATION: *Where or how does the value of advice take shape between students at your school? What haikus might your students craft on giving or receiving advice?*

_____

_____

_____

_____

_____

_____

Another haiku:

My daughter offers

Much perspective for my growth

Her love inspires change.

REFLECT: *What would friends, family, and students observe or say about your ability to give and receive advice?*

_____

_____

_____

_____

_____

Today, which core assumption did you lean into deeply and how did that feel? Was there a core assumption that you struggled with and what could support look like tomorrow?

1 The true self in everyone is good, wise, and powerful.

7 We need practices to build habits of living from the core self.

2 The world is profoundly interconnected.

6 Human beings are holistic.

3 All human beings have a deep desire to be in a good relationship.

5 Everything we need to make positive change is already here.

4 All human beings have gifts, and everyone is needed for what they bring.

For me, some of the greatest learning and revelation occurs when my instincts and internal compass mesh with advice I receive through meaningful relationship. And too, there are sources of information and learning in everything from music and poetry to simply pausing to observe the ecosystem of passing time between classes (or, say, engaging in a workbook about RP). Lean into the graphic below to consider sources and spaces of advice related to restorative practices. Where might they align and fuse?

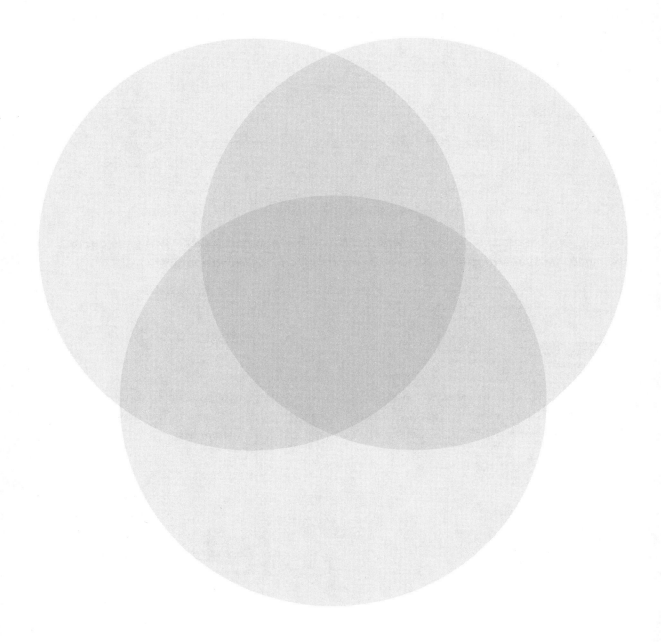

Restorative Practices at School

More Wisdom: When *Advice* Takes the Form of Profound Example

Jim Yang and Shawn Davenport have been the restorative practices leaders at Farnsworth Aerospace Upper School in St. Paul for the past three years. Together, their remarkable blend of passion, patience, and persistence has prompted many stories of growth and good. They also have established themselves as consummate restorative hosts to guest after learning guest from St. Paul Public Schools neighbors and from around the state and country.

Shawn Davenport identifies as African American and uses he/him/his pronouns. Jim Yang identifies as Hmong American and uses he/him/his pronouns. Here's what they shared in regard to RP in schools.

On their opening learning in restorative practices:

Shawn: My learning with restorative practices is that it's more than just repairing harm. It's a way of being. Removing assumptions by building authentic relationships within the community, school, and classroom.

Jim: Grounding. I feel I have been doing restorative work without the formal training or terminology. My experience and training in restorative practices has given me a different perspective on my life, my relationships, and my career as an educator.

What are the core values or reflections you have experienced through restorative practices?

Shawn: With the implementation of restorative practices I've seen staff and students become more relational. More trusting of one another, which has made it easier to communicate and iron out differences. Both students and staff have learned to be more reflective of themselves. Taking more of an ownership of how they speak and act toward one another.

Jim: My work in RP has shifted and shaped countless relationships with students. I am just thankful to have an opportunity to work with amazing and gifted young people. Listening to their stories and blessed to be in their presence, I feel I've learned more from students than they can ever learn from me as an educator. For that, I am truly privileged to be in my role in the community.

Offerings and advice to educators and friends newer to RP:

Shawn: My advice would be to first be reflective of your own beliefs, biases being brought into a space. Start small and take your time with staff and students. Focus on building community. Be prepared to fail, but don't quit. Be reflective and learn from mistakes. Consistency and repetition are key. Also, while circles are important, they're not the be-all, end-all. How are you building relationships day to day? How are voices being heard, students being recognized?

Jim: Slow the process and breathe. It begins with you. Take time to understand yourself, your bias, your history, your trauma, and how you show up every day. Then and only then will you truly understand and see RP manifest into something magnificent.

REFLECT: *There's no shortage of books filled with content to meet learning curiosity. For you, what was the content of Shawn and Jim's testimony, and what might you feel newly curious about?*

_____

_____

_____

_____

_____

_____

_____

What were your learning takeaways from their shared perspectives?

_____

_____

_____

_____

_____

_____

The Wisdom of Youth: My Son, Quinn, as Good, Wise, and Powerful

I've lived with a middle schooler for the past two years. I generally sit in astonished awe of his person-hood. The whirl of being witness to his learning runs the restorative gamut from, "I am still learning about that!" to spectacular incredulity.

Note this scaffolded learning approach he took with a friend when introducing the concept of chocolate babka to a friend: "You know what a loaf of bread is, right?"

To which I, Mom, gasped and said, "Quinn! He knows what a loaf of bread is!" and we all chuckled.

Or this video game banter of anticipation: "I need only two more kills for something special."

And, as a multiracial young man, Quinn has said, "I am the biggest outsider of all at school."

As an educator and mother, I know that I need to slow down in order to fully appreciate Quinn's good-ness, wisdom, and power.

REFLECT: *What might Quinn's remarks above prompt for you?*

_____

_____

_____

_____

_____

What language and words of our youth have steeped and stayed with you and why?

_____

_____

_____

_____

_____

What supports the slowdown needed to listen deeply to the wisdom of our youth?

_____

_____

_____

_____

_____

What is the value of "slowing down" in education? What might be another way to rethink the language of slowing down?

_____

_____

_____

_____

_____

In a classroom?

_____

_____

_____

_____

_____

In a moment of dysregulation?

_____

_____

_____

_____

Another Remarkable Restorative Story

Lifting our true selves, our goodness, and our power through shared stories *with* those who love us best is a big part of restorative practices.

Here's a story from one of St. Paul's middle school restorative practices pilot sites:

There was a young person that was being seriously bullied in class, so he and his family came in. There were two other students [involved] and I was able to get in all of their families. It came out in preconferencing that they actually had all faced bullying at different times. So, we were able to do a restorative circle, talking about what happened, talking about that hurt and the woundedness everyone had felt. It was really beautiful. It happened to all be mothers, and seeing the mothers collectively love on this one student that had been harmed while also holding accountable and at the same time loving their own students was really beautiful and I think really transformative. Everyone left crying, but also left with these three young people being really strong with each other and in restored relationship. Moving on and out of that, all three mothers wanted to be part of antibullying efforts at this school, saying, "Could we do more of this? We have to deal with things this way." I was really proud that the mother of the bullied student moved from, "I want these students suspended immediately" to "How do we actually solve this?"

REFLECT: *How does this story move and affect you?*

_____

_____

_____

_____

_____

_____

_____

_____

Throughout this text, "Hurt people hurt people" has surfaced as a meaningful anchor for restorative practices work. How might a school's approach to bullying shift through a restorative lens on what all members of the community might need?

_____

_____

_____

_____

_____

_____

_____

_____

From your lens, how might you grow the expression "hurt people hurt people?"

_____

_____

_____

_____

_____

_____

_____

_____

_____

The story on page 89 illustrates the value and critical importance of preconferencing before a restorative process that seeks to problem solve or attend to harm. Preconferencing also nurtures the practice of mapping the history of harm. For example, often what I would witness of student behavior in a classroom had origin from their morning at home or friendship strife from the previous class period. Use the open space below to map a recent experience in which you harmed someone.

A (Consistent) Return to Self

The world is profoundly interconnected, for real.

I was adopted from Korea when I was five months old. When I think about the idea that our world is interconnected, my origin always comes to mind and a restorative faith that my biological mother thinks of me from time to time, just as she floats through my heart and mind. In Korea a woman held me in her womb and nurtured me as best she knew how. And in May of 1976 she drew on every ounce of her will and strength to say a forever farewell to me. In rural Minnesota, a family—my adoptive-family-to-be—craved a way to fulfill their dream of having children. So, spirited by love and possibility, my life took shape. Now the mother of two of my own children, whose personalities you've had the opportunity to glimpse throughout these pages, I know better the aching loss my birth mother must have felt as any distance from my own children means a different way of breathing.

Last year, the editor of Living Justice Press, a remarkable and loving local publishing house of restorative texts (quite literally, someone's home) gifted me with a copy of *Circle Forward*, from where we draw the Seven Core Assumptions, which had been translated into Korean. I have many copies of *Circle Forward* in English, but for me, the most magical one is the version I cannot read. The magic of knowing that circles are being held in Korea is a divine way to know that my work and care are mirrored across an ocean. I have origin and I am connected.

For the past five years, during the first week in July, I've taught the self-esteem class at Camp Choson, a Korean Cultural Camp, which radiates welcome and love for me and my family. This year, while leading the campers, a gorgeous assortment of adoptees and folks lovingly in relationship with Korean adoption, in a circle, I placed the Korean copy of *Circle Forward* on my centerpiece, and the loving eyes that fell upon it as I explained its meaning were a window of connection.

REFLECT: *Consider how something in your life deeply links and loops to meaningful connection with others.*

_____

_____

_____

_____

_____

How do you believe your classroom or school creates such links and loops for your scholars?

_____

_____

_____

_____

_____

From my tale, I looped my origin of place and language, giving back to the community I come from and recognizing the random acts of kindness in my life. How is your classroom or school a flexible space for such themes from your own life?

_____

_____

_____

_____

_____

Healthy Relationships Look All Kinds of Ways

We are always observing relationships.

Perhaps the very healthiest relationship I had as a young person was that between my own mind and the pages of a good book. That sanctuary space to observe the nature of others without worry that I would be caught staring awkwardly was such a spacious way to consider what made people speak, act, and engage as they did.

Whether it's a character from a book, a recurring figure in a TV show or movie, or a public figure, our core human value of curiosity seeks to know people dimensionally.

REFLECT: *Consider examples of characters in books, TV shows, or movies, or even public figures, modeling the integrity of "All human beings have a deep desire to be in a good relationship." Who were those characters and people that struck you, and what did they teach you about good relationships?*

Our Capacity to Repair

Every hour of the school day, young people are navigating dozens of relationships—with their peers, with their educators, and with those they have relationships with outside school. For many young people, connection to others and relationship-building takes place as members of a team, a way to be valued both for their skills and their personhood.

Here is a story from one of our restorative practices middle schools:

We had a situation on our basketball team in which a phone went missing. Instead of launching an investigation aimed at finding out who did it and punishing that person, we held a circle to talk about it. Through that process, the young man who took the phone took ownership of his actions and admitted it to the team. He returned the phone to its owner. To the student's surprise, the team decided together that they wanted him to remain on the team.

REFLECT: *What happened in this story that feels familiar or unlike how your school processes harm?*

_____

_____

_____

_____

_____

What about the team's resolution feels good, wise, and powerful?

_____

_____

_____

_____

_____

When do you shift in your personal and professional practice away from believing that you can make it right—however time-consuming or uncomfortable—to the very opposite idea, that harm means you need to be separated from something or someone of value?

_____

_____

_____

_____

_____

_____

Today, which core assumption did you lean into deeply and how did that feel? Was there a core assumption that you struggled with and what could support look like tomorrow?

1 The true self in everyone is good, wise, and powerful.

7 We need practices to build habits of living from the core self.

2 The world is profoundly interconnected.

6 Human beings are holistic.

3 All human beings have a deep desire to be in a good relationship.

5 Everything we need to make positive change is already here.

4 All human beings have gifts, and everyone is needed for what they bring.

It Takes Time to Build, Nurture, and Sustain Healthy Relationships

I love greeting cards. I take pictures of ones I think are clever and text them to friends instead of buying them and mailing them; it's a ridiculously abbreviated act of generosity and a pattern real to busy lives filled with good intention. And it means that I pretty regularly sit with a gentle sense of guilt and disconnect from those I love most.

In the tale below, youth leaders at one of St. Paul's restorative practices high schools remind me to take such time and make space for the full form of my values and desire to be in good relationships.

> At the beginning of this school year, there were some fights that happened. In our senior leadership class of 36 students, we were able to do some processing in terms of what does that mean and how does that affect us. And that spurred "Sit with me" and "Talk with me" initiatives. They said, "Well, some of the younger kids don't think anybody understands them." So, they went to some training with our social workers about leading peer groups. The "Talk with me" initiative is so kids can call them, send them social media notes, and then they'll sit down and talk. And they started a "Sit with us" group in the cafeteria. Every couple of weeks they pull some tables aside and they say, "Come sit with us." So, they're trying to actually pull the community together. These ideas came out of circle conversations. So, it wasn't accidental.

REFLECT: *When were you recently invited to sit with someone for such a vital conversation?*

_____

_____

_____

_____

_____

The invitation for this page is to create a list of 10 folks for whom you wish or need to make space and time to sit and talk with.

I commit to a Sit with Me, Talk with Me window with _____ because

_____ .

I commit to a Sit with Me, Talk with Me window with _____ because

_____ .

I commit to a Sit with Me, Talk with Me window with _____ because

_____ .

I commit to a Sit with Me, Talk with Me window with _____ because

_____ .

I commit to a Sit with Me, Talk with Me window with _____ because

_____ .

I commit to a Sit with Me, Talk with Me window with _____ because

_____ .

I commit to a Sit with Me, Talk with Me window with _____ because

_____ .

REFLECT: *How might you bring such an idea to your staff or classroom?*

_____

_____

_____

_____

_____

What might a Sit with Me, Talk with Me space look, sound, or feel like and how might its installation incorporate the values it seeks to breathe?

_____

_____

_____

_____

_____

On the next page, use the Seven Core Assumptions of RP for your planning. How might the work and such a project consistently anchor back to these tenets?

_____

_____

_____

_____

_____

Example:

The true self in everyone is good, wise, and powerful: Every young person has the capacity to be present and to be a listener to others. How does such a space empower adults and young people to gain healthy skills?

CORE ASSUMPTION	HOW TO PLAN FOR A SIT WITH ME, TALK WITH ME SPACE
The true self in everyone is good, wise, and powerful.	
The world is profoundly interconnected.	
All human beings have a deep desire to be in a good relationship.	
All human beings have gifts, and everyone is needed for what they bring.	
Everything we need to make positive change is already here.	
Human beings are holistic.	
We need practices to build habits of living from the core self.	

Sharing Space with Our Families

We need practices to build habits of living from our core selves *with our students' families.*

Each year, when it came to parent/family–teacher conference season, I experienced a gentle sort of dread. And it wasn't because of the longer work day (though that's real) or because of putting on my twice-yearly conference dress (again, still a thing). It was because I wasn't sure that with each family I could state with unequivocal truth that I had done my best to accelerate their child's learning, and, more vitally, that I knew them fully and what they needed as scholars and as people.

I know this: Even though I always led conferences with a story of celebration and acknowledgment of their child's awesomeness and then segued into spaces for growth, I did not lead by way of coming to know the parents or family and their hopes and wishes for their child. I did not invite, "What is a value you hold fast to when sending your child to school each day?" or "What is one value you believe is critical I lean into to best serve and learn with your child?"

REFLECT: *What values guide your family engagement work and why?*

Family

I offer this tale from Terri Jackson, principal of Nokomis North Montessori Elementary School in St. Paul, Minnesota, a restorative practices pilot site in year two of their whole-school implementation work. Terri identifies as Chinese American and uses she/her/hers pronouns. The values Terri holds most dear in her restorative story are kindness, compassion, growth, vulnerability, inclusiveness, and love.

> [A] heartwarming story which will always be etched in my heart took place in my first year as an RP coordinator. I had asked for a few teacher volunteers to hold teacher/parent conferences in circle. After much thoughtful planning, we decided to start with this prompt, "What are you most proud of about your child?" One of the parents was silent for some time and then began to cry. He then said, "Nobody has ever asked me that before about my kids!" He beamed as he shared about his child, and was so grateful that he was able to have a space to share about what was important to him about his son!

REFLECT: *What values do you hear most profoundly from parents and family members?*

_____

_____

_____

_____

_____

_____

_____

_____

_____

_____

What supports your relationship to those values amid the many pressures and responsibilities within an educator's day?

_____

_____

_____

_____

_____

_____

_____

_____

Another tale from Terri about the value and meaning to families learning from and with their scholars about restorative practices:

> A parent from one of our parent circles shared about her family's Christmas Eve celebration. The extended family was about to gather at the table for Christmas dinner and her kindergarten son said, "Stop, everyone! Before we eat, we are going to share." He held a stuffed animal and explained that it was a talking piece. "When you have the talking piece, you can share, but if you don't have the talking piece, you need to be listening. Everyone will get a turn because we will pass the talking piece around."
>
> He then proceeded to ask the whole group this prompt: "What is your favorite Christmas tradition?"
>
> All the adults in the room were astonished at the brilliance of how such a youngster could bring forth such connections using the tools he had learned in his RP circles in class as a kindergartner! And this will be their tradition going forward as a family.

REFLECT: *What happened in this story that stands out to you?*

_____

_____

_____

_____

_____

How would you feel if a student returned from winter break with such a tale?

_____

_____

_____

_____

What practices and rituals in your classroom consistently invite such a celebratory exchange between school and home?

_____

_____

_____

_____

(Restorative) Movement and Space Matter

When I student taught in the fall of 1998, I was very, very green. Nylons-and-heels, new-to-the-profession sort of green, as opposed to a dedicated-black-stretchy-pants, cute-tennies sort of educator of today's dress code. Spatially, I spent the first week of class teaching within a two-by-five space, moving to the left and right and occasionally mixing it up with the infrequent step forward. My body deeply held my nervousness and not appreciating that my stillness was, at best, awkward, I could not move for fear of "dropping" or misplacing my content.

Ever so gently, my cooperating teacher shared her observation of my geographically contained teaching and urged me to move. Thank goodness! From then on, I strove to move about the room and to know the classroom and learners from different perspectives. To this day, movement when I facilitate professional development always empowers a shift in my perspective and energy, and reminds me to empower the scholars to stretch and move too.

And, from a vulnerable space, I was absolutely coached to use my proximity to students as a deterrent for off-task behavior. The idea of lingering nearby, peering over, or frequently visiting scholars meant one thing to me—I was redirecting, and through a restorative lens, I now see how it was so much more.

I wonder, what did students notice of my movement and where I stopped or wandered by? Where did I most often pause to engage, when was I likely to keep going, and what did that look like from a racial equity lens? Where were restorative spaces of relationship-building, and where were spaces I entered from a belief space that "little work was getting done"?

I believe that moving within our classrooms prompts a healthy, energized version of ourselves, and it was imperative for me to examine how I used proximity and movement to reveal my bias and my preference, and to acknowledge how and when I carried an energy of restorative belief versus one of deficit and concern.

Exercise: Using the blank square below, draw out the design of your classroom space. Then, using a different color or pencil, track where your movements take you. If you're feeling really ambitious, use a different color for each class period.

REFLECT: *What do your steps show you about your practice?*

_____

_____

_____

_____

_____

Restorative Practices at School

How do those pathways differ by hour and time of day?

_____

_____

_____

_____

_____

_____

What do you notice about your patterns of movement and stillness from a lens of equity?

_____

_____

_____

_____

_____

_____

EDUCATOR APPLICATION: *What might support different pathways of movement in your classroom or school that are predictable, equitable, and healthy for students and yourself?*

_____

_____

_____

_____

_____

_____

Many classrooms in schools include spaces in the classroom for students to "take a break." These spots in classrooms are sometimes described as regulation stations, peace spots, time-out chairs, and when partnered with another classroom, they become known as the "buddy room."

REFLECTION: *How did you come of age to understand what it meant to take a break or have a time-out?*

_____

_____

_____

_____

_____

Where and how did you learn about self-regulation?

_____

_____

_____

_____

What are your current habits that ensure you see a "break" as healthy as opposed to punitive or a judgment?

_____

_____

_____

_____

_____

When do your students and colleagues take breaks?

_____

_____

_____

_____

_____

What is understood about that self-advocacy?

_____

_____

_____

_____

_____

What bias might our system hold and what personal bias might you have internalized about habits of self-care, sensory breaks, and a restorative response to others?

_____

_____

_____

_____

_____

Exercise: In the space below, design an ideal "take a break space" for yourself. What would it involve? What is the goal or intention of this space? What about this space would be restorative and healthy? How would the space accomplish its intent?

Our Inherent Capacity for Growth

We learn balance when we stumble.

Here's a story from one of our restorative practices middle schools:

> There was an incident on a bus and one of our students that's been with us for three years came into the office. The first words out of his mouth were, "I know you're going to suspend me, I get it. Let's just call my dad." So immediately, we just said, "No, no, you're not going to get suspended." This was all of three or four weeks into the school year, and he had been doing community-building circles in homeroom every single day, so he knew how to do circle. We told him we were going to do circle.

> Our coordinator did an amazing job preparing him for what to expect, that it would be different from our community-building circles. She asked if he wanted an advocate in circle and he invited an adult in the building with whom he has a close relationship. This young man who has a history of significant behavior in our building was able to own his behavior, understand the pain he created, and reduce his referrals to the office by more than 60 percent in the year since circle happened.

Restorative practices invite a way of processing and reflection that differ from a traditional, "Do you know what rule you broke? Why did you do that? Are you aware of the consequences for your actions?" Instead, the explorative questions invite first a student's description and understanding, how they felt, and what they believe they might or could do to make things right. Rather than requesting a student speak first to what they knew but didn't follow (a rule) or asking a student to defend or explain something they might not be able to, what about leaning first into what a student knows might make a difference?

Below are the restorative questions applied to the tale above.

REFLECT: *What happened in this story?*

_____

_____

_____

_____

_____

What do you think the student felt after their choice?

_____

_____

_____

_____

_____

What did they feel after the circle?

_____

_____

_____

_____

_____

What did they do to make things right?

_____

_____

_____

_____

_____

How might they feel about themselves following such a restorative process?

_____

_____

_____

_____

_____

Consider how harm is processed in your own community, for youth and for adults. What does it look and sound like:

When an adult is connected to or experiences harm?	When a young person is connected to or experiences harm?

The restorative questions invite the following exploration: What happened? What were you thinking or feeling then? What have you been thinking about or feeling since then? Who has been affected and how? What do you think you need to do to make things right? What might others need to do to make things right?

_____

_____

How do your reflections in the table above mirror or differ from the restorative questions as a means to process, reflect, and work toward repair?

_____

_____

We Need Reminders of Our True, Good Selves

A story from one of our elementary restorative practices sites:

I did a professional development one morning and the opening was about a cultural group that, when somebody does something egregious in their town, they circle up around the person and tell them everything that is good about them until the person believes it, whether it's two days or two weeks or whatever. And I said, "The student that drives you the most crazy, couldn't you put him or her in the middle of the room and have everybody tell them something good about them?" And the next day a teacher said, "I did it. Not only that, he needed it twice in the same day and we gathered together for him twice in the same day." And she said, "It was beautiful and these third graders had the most thoughtful, deep, true connective statements to say about this child and just transformed his life that day." And now they're all signing up so she's doing the entire class.

REFLECT: *What happened in this story?*

_____

_____

_____

_____

_____

What do you think the student felt about hearing from his peers about his inherent worth and goodness?

_____

_____

_____

_____

_____

How might the class have felt?

_____

_____

_____

_____

_____

What feels right about this for the individual student, the educator, and the community?

_____

_____

_____

_____

_____

How might the community feel after such a practice? After the practice is normed?

_____

_____

_____

_____

_____

_____

_____

All Voices

Restorative practices are about all voices being given the space to name their truth with love and respect, and to elevate conversations otherwise internalized.

Here's a story from one of our restorative practices high schools:

One of the things that happens here, with the very racially diverse community—majority Asian population, mostly Hmong—is that for our black students there's definitely a sentiment of "There's no room for us, there's no value for us." So, when we do circles and talk about fights or we talk about the impact of Black History Month or lack of culture or diversity, we've heard our black students be able to voice, "Hey, we want a space in this particular place. And we want to have our experiences valued and celebrated."

So, I've heard students be able to talk about that in front of their peers and then I've heard other nonblack students say, "Yes, that's something we believe in too." I think that was really powerful for students to be able to hear that. From my perspective, I don't think there's a lot of cross dialogue happening between communities of color.

REFLECT: *At present, what do conversations about race and equity look, sound, and feel like in your classroom and school community?*

_____

_____

_____

_____

_____

_____

_____

_____

_____

What values guide both intentional and responsive conversations about race and equity? What supports the invitation, inclusion, and safety for all voices?

_____

_____

_____

_____

_____

_____

_____

_____

_____

How does the story on page 116 illustrate how restorative practices might empower a different way of creating an anti-racist, antibias classroom or school community?

_____

_____

_____

_____

_____

_____

_____

_____

Equity, Always

How might the Seven Core Assumptions guide and support conversations about race and equity beyond the current habits and practices in your community? How do they already align with current ritual?

CORE ASSUMPTION	HOW MIGHT DIALOGUE ABOUT RACE AND EQUITY SHIFT AND BE SUPPORTED BY RESTORATIVE PRACTICES?
The true self in everyone is good, wise, and powerful.	
The world is profoundly interconnected.	
All human beings have a deep desire to be in a good relationship.	
All human beings have gifts, and everyone is needed for what they bring.	
Everything we need to make positive change is already here.	
Human beings are holistic.	
We need practices to build habits of living from the core self.	

Restorative Practices at School

A Way of Being and Ways of Practice

Restorative practices are a way of being first, emerging from a place of belief. And then, they become a way of being in practice.

The following are two stories from one of our restorative practices elementary schools:

I walk in to support one of our fifth-grade classes when they have a sub. She is reading the paper and she says, "It says something about a centerpiece." And one of the students goes, "I got it." And he gets out the basket with their centerpiece and lays out the centerpiece that they created with their paper plates. Then she goes, "What's all that?" And one of the other students chimes in and says, "Those are the values we bring to school every day. Those are the things we try to uphold every day in our learning." And then somebody takes the talking piece and asks them a question for the morning and runs the entire circle. So for those big kids to say, like, "Yep, this is what we are about and this is what we do and regardless of who the teacher might be standing in there, this is what we are about."

***

One of my most joyous days was while visiting a first-grade teacher. Four students came over and said, "You don't have to have a circle or anything, we already did! We used the questions and see over there is our centerpiece and it's OK we used your pointer talking piece and we are all fixed now, we feel OK, and we are all going to play in a circle at recess to celebrate!" (The teacher and I had not even been aware of the conflict or the circle as we had been observing other students....) It had become their norm, their way!

REFLECT: *What did you notice was happening in these two stories?*

_____

_____

_____

_____

_____

How might it feel for young people to welcome new educators with such agency?

_____

_____

_____

_____

_____

What might it feel like to a young person to restoratively problem-solve?

_____

_____

_____

_____

_____

How might the class have felt in either situation?

_____

_____

_____

_____

_____

What feels right about this for individual students, educators, and the community?

_____

_____

_____

_____

_____

Today, which core assumption did you lean into deeply and how did that feel? Was there a core assumption that you struggled with and what could support look like tomorrow?

1 The true self in everyone is good, wise, and powerful.

7 We need practices to build habits of living from the core self.

2 The world is profoundly interconnected.

6 Human beings are holistic.

3 All human beings have a deep desire to be in a good relationship.

5 Everything we need to make positive change is already here.

4 All human beings have gifts, and everyone is needed for what they bring.

We Are the Work

All human beings have gifts, and everyone is needed for what they bring.

From the beginning, Maxfield Elementary School, one of our restorative practices pilot sites, has been blessed to be collaboratively led by Fallon Henderson. Fallon identifies as an African American woman who uses she/her/hers pronouns.

Distinguished in her practice and personhood, Fallon, like our community of restorative practitioners, lives in the truth of how we have been measured and measure ourselves. And she is gifted. And needed.

In the beginning stages of becoming a restorative practices lead I struggled with believing in what I had been and who I have been all this time. Was it enough to be deserving of this title? I would always question my being and my interactions and relationships with students and colleagues. "Am I doing the right thing?" I would say, or "Am I upholding what others' thoughts and opinions and expectations of my actions accurate for this position [should be]?" I still don't know to this day if I am. However, as the years pass I gain more knowledge and experience, and I realize I have just become more rich. All this time I have been creating change through my life journey by sharing my stories. Rather than being joy or pain I was just simply being, and all along that was everything that was needed.

REFLECT: *What about Fallon's story is rooted in a truth students, educators, and community hold?*

_____

_____

_____

_____

_____

_____

_____

_____

What does it mean to be a learning leader of something like restorative practices?

_____

_____

_____

_____

_____

_____

_____

_____

_____

How might you narrate your own way of being in education, both in joy and pain?

_____

_____

_____

_____

_____

_____

_____

_____

_____

_____

Compassionate, Healthy Accountability

Creating personal and professional restorative next steps should bear kindly your hopes, needs, and critical supports. Nancy Riestenberg, restorative specialist for the Minnesota Department of Education, guided me toward the language of restorative agreements for self and school. For example, can I commit to counting back from 10 in a moment of difficulty or conflict with a colleague? Will I commit to naming and posting the good, wise, and powerful traits of all students in my classroom by fall break? Could I begin all dialogue—when harm has occurred—by grounding myself in those truths? To meet such goals, who will be my support, a reflective partner or ally, and celebrate my hiccups and progress?

As you near the close of this book, think about how these core tenets of RP might hold you deeply accountable and simultaneously support you.

CORE ASSUMPTION	HOW DOES THIS HOLD YOU ACCOUNTABLE/SUPPORT YOU?
The true self in everyone is good, wise, and powerful.	Example: I've attended many trainings on RP and sat in hundreds of circles. I hold myself accountable to that learning and the integrity of sharing with others such "content" with grace. I must hold space for other educators who have not experienced such RP saturation with patience and faith in their goodness, wisdom, and power.
The true self in everyone is good, wise, and powerful.	
The world is profoundly interconnected.	
All human beings have a deep desire to be in a good relationship.	

CORE ASSUMPTION	HOW DOES THIS HOLD YOU ACCOUNTABLE/SUPPORT YOU?
All human beings have gifts, and everyone is needed for what they bring.	
Everything we need to make positive change is already here.	
Human beings are holistic.	
We need practices to build habits of living from the core self.	

Expansive, Inclusive, True Definition

Restorative practices are core to our humanity. Necessary for healthy relationships, they are both flexible and unrelenting in the commitment to a way of being in community.

Toward the beginning of the book, I offered several ways in which people seek to describe and capture the essence of restorative practices.

In St. Paul, we hold the following to be true:

- We believe that learning is relational and our schools should be places of engagement and accountability achieved with students.

- We focus most of our effort on establishing strong, inclusive relationships within our communities through regular community-building circles.

- We engage students by connecting to their lived experiences through content circles, which evolve from an understanding and practice of community-building circles.

- We aim to empower, understand, provide support, and create accountability for all who had a role in harm that occurs in our communities, including historical harm, so that relationships are restored.

REFLECT: *When you read the language above, how does this sync with the impressions of RP you had before reading this book?*

How does it mirror or contrast with your classroom or school's culture and values?

_____

_____

_____

_____

_____

_____

_____

_____

On page 5 you were introduced to the expression "I am the work" and invited to craft caring commitments to your values, practice, and story. Below, craft a community-driven "My school is the work" piece. Sentence starters have been provided.

My school is the work _____

My school is the work _____

Being the work _____

My school is the work _____

My school is the work _____

My school is the work _____

My school is the work _____

Challenge and Possibility

A story of "Never Have I Ever" is from the incomparable Kurt Blomberg, the restorative practices lead for one of our high schools. Kurt identifies as Korean American and uses he/him/his pronouns.

Never Have I Ever

In a professional development training, teachers gave me 112 reasons why they would not do a circle in their classroom. After hearing them out, I asked them, "What might you need to make a circle happen?" It was time to go and I didn't hear their answers. The next day, one educator requested that I come into their sixth-hour class to observe their circle. They started with a movement activity in which students were moving around and having small interactions with one another. Ten minutes later the teacher called them to circle up. They asked the following questions:

- Have you been sick in the last six months?

- When you get sick, who is the person who takes care of you?

- As we know, Western medicine isn't the only way people can heal themselves. How does your family take care of you when you are sick?

The variety of responses was one thing. The most notable thing I observed was the level of engagement students had with each other. There was a genuine desire to share and listen to one another. I observed two occasions when students corrected other students to ensure that the person who had the talking piece was listened to. The teacher wrapped up the circle with a personal story about health and how this related to their larger unit of viruses.

After the class, the teacher said, "OK, there's something to build off." I simply replied, "Yes." There are many things that have been done to educators that prevent them from showing up as their authentic selves.

REFLECT: *What happened in the story Kurt shared?*

_____

_____

_____

_____

_____

Where might the resistance to restorative practices work emerge from?

_____

_____

_____

_____

What harms live in educators' everyday professional responsibilities and realities?

_____

_____

_____

_____

How do we heal as a community from those challenges?

_____

_____

_____

_____

_____

Kurt offers these prompts: How might we, who are responsible for the growth and coaching of our colleagues, model and hold their truths to offer the opportunity for tectonic shifts to happen within their practices and hearts?

_____

_____

_____

_____

_____

What is freeing about listing 112 reasons why circles or restorative practices might not work? What agency might that inspire to say aloud your worries or sense of barrier?

Celebrating Self (You)

Using the story boxes below, say what this workbook experience has been like for you through the lens of values (e.g., the value of learning, beginning, struggle, confusion, stretch)?

Your Awesomeness!

Every day, you are authoring for young people the lessons linked to learning standards and, just as vitally, modeling a way of being. Through your work in this book, you have been authoring chapters of your restorative story. (Hurray! And you are awesome!)

Growing up, I was introduced by my teachers to plot charts and the arc of story. In these lessons, the grid below was used to illustrate the beginning of a relationship and the introduction to characters, their growing conflict and tension, often brought about by a third party, and how things came to a climax or breaking point. From that, things "worked out" or resolved themselves. How we learned to map stories and think about narrative was through this singular, mysterious lens of closure.

Name: _____   Date: _____

Title: _____

Directions:

enter text here

enter text here

enter text here

enter text here

enter text here

enter text here

enter text here

REFLECT: *What about this kind of "plot chart" feels limiting? What about this kind of chart feels true?*

_____

_____

_____

_____

_____

_____

_____

_____

_____

_____

About 10 years ago, I attended the Absent Narratives Learning Cohort at the Minnesota Humanities Center and was introduced to a very different way to think about story, both my own and those stories I was witness to.

From those lessons, the circle that begins internally and moves outward was introduced with the language of an indigenous story circle. And this was so, so freeing! For years, I had been trying to pinion students into the typical, dominant-culture version of a plot chart, and when students would point out a nuance or complexity, I could only affably acknowledge their wisdom. The chart was the chart.

The idea that I am creating a whirl of connected story, in which each new relationship, experience, and learning is anchored within my collective history—how marvelous and rooted!

In the exercise on page 131, your creativity and artistry was welcomed via a value storyboard of sorts. For this activity, lean into the circle crafted below to capture the experience of exploring your restorative practices story. Where do you hope to go with restorative practices centering your values, your relationships and community, your hopes and aspirations?

And finally, what if your classroom or school crafted such a story together? What if a wall or bulletin board or space held the emerging story of values and relationship for your community?

Self Story Mapping

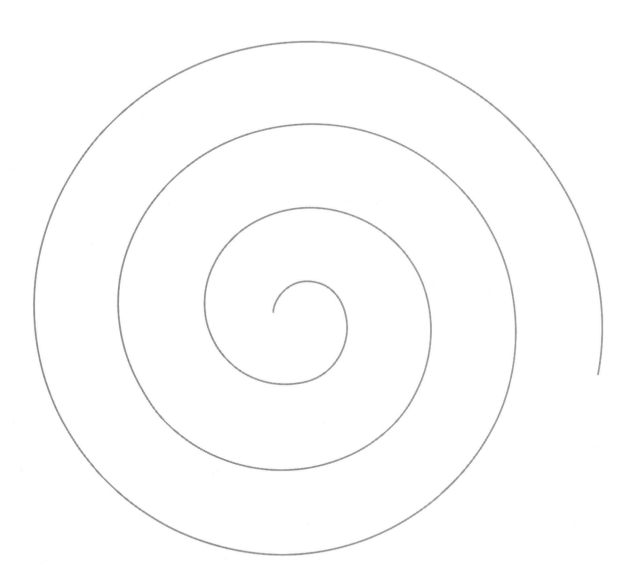

Restorative Practices at School

Community Story Mapping

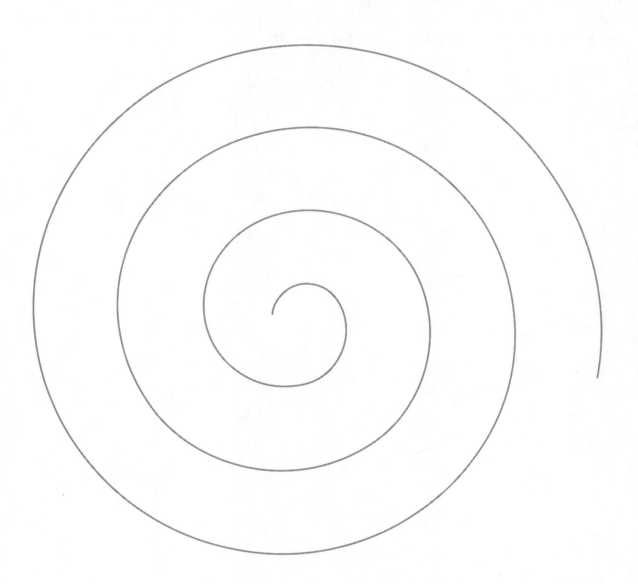

Defining Restorative Practices for Myself

Phew! Because you've (hopefully) stretched the binding to accommodate your progress through this book, there is much to celebrate and potentially summarize. Use the space below for such notes, imagery, questions, and beyond. Heck, use this as draft space for a "Dear Becky" email with your wonderings.

Gratitude

In January of 2019, when I embarked on the planning, drafting, percolating moments of assembling this restorative experience, I jotted down this partial poem.

Authoring

I wonder if authoring might be like mothering-to-be, a blend of gestation and food cravings.

It certainly must be about surviving and trimming the hedges around thriving.

Perhaps authoring is like Lily's free-choice baking, a floury haze of messy good intentions.

Maybe authoring is like nearly kissing—the frustrating, tantalizing, lip-biting anticipation of meaningful connection.

Somewhere in my heart I believe my authorship has always been an inadequate compass,

A creaky, tilting globe with language too tiny to read,

Has been latitude and lassitude instead of intersecting forces of production.

I wonder if authoring is too front and center and not enough stage manager for me.

Perhaps I am meant for footnotes and margins.

And in the closing hours before hitting send/submit on the first complete draft of this text, I'm holding these truths around when you restoratively author sh**....

For as long as I can remember, I've internalized the limited idea that someone like Albert Einstein, or a similarly extolled smart white man, believed that we only use 15 percent of our brain.

I defy that science. He wasn't working in education. Nor living in the world as a woman of color. Or seeking to decolonize his parenthood. I've internalized the limited idea that we only use a small portion of our brain.

As a Korean American woman, a single mother, an educator, an adoptee, a survivor of much harm, and an effusive wordsmith, I am using every ounce of my dang brain to serve and puzzle my way through a messy, amazing world. I lean into love and patience like a blended CrossFit of social emotional learning and racial equity.

I am deeply, marvelously imperfect and still, today, a humble, grateful lowercase *author* of some hard heart work.

If you liked any part of this book at all, reach out. My emails won't disappoint.

About the Author

Becky McCammon is the restorative practices program coordinator at St. Paul Public Schools. She loves haiku poems, effusive text messaging, and, most especially, having been a middle and high school English teacher for 14 years. At the core of her joy and education practice with young people and adults is a belief in our binding, beautiful stories. Over the years, Becky has collected a happy assortment of lanyards and canvas bags from conferences around the country, where she has offered perspective and learning about racial equity, restorative practices, and the critical role of educator unions in supporting healthy schools for students, staff, families, and community.

As mom to Quinn and Lily, Becky prides herself on everyday learning and the critical role of humor, forgiveness, and just the right balance of yes and no. She does not serve enough vegetables to her children but asks plenty of feeling questions. Becky supports and learns alongside her peers at schools in St. Paul, Minnesota, as a circle keeper, coach, ally, leader, and expert in restorative practices.